Summary of

Presence

: Bringing Your Boldest Self to Your Biggest Challenges

by Amy Cuddy

: This is a quick read summary based on the novel

"Presence"

by Amy Cuddy

D0067480

TABLE OF CONTENTS

INTRODUCTION

Amy Cuddy is known worldwide for her 2012 TED talk titled "Your Body Language Shapes Who You Are," which remains one of the most-viewed TED talks to date. The material from her talk is part of a larger body of her research on body language which reveals that it is possible to change how we perceive ourselves, how others perceive us, and even our own body chemistry by simply altering our body positions from ones of powerlessness to ones of power and presence. From this research was born Cuddy's book, *Presence*.

Cuddy is a social psychologist and professor at Harvard Business School. Her research focuses on nonverbal behavior and its influence and has been published in some of the most respected academic journals as well as other major publications including *The New York Times* and *The Wall Street Journal*.

In *Presence* Cuddy teaches readers about power, body language, and the state of presence. Most people experience high-stress, high-stakes situations in their lives. In these circumstances, when we most need to be confident and capable, we most often feel inadequate and powerless. By understanding how to achieve a state of presence, we can alter our behavior and, as a result, the outcome of these challenging situations.

Cuddy teaches readers how to access our own personal power and achieve what she calls "presence" – a state in which we experience comfortable confidence and worry less about how others perceive us and more about how we perceive ourselves. While the techniques and tools necessary to achieve presence are somewhat complex, they are also practical, simple to execute, and accessible to anyone. We already possess the basic tools we need – such as breathing – to nudge ourselves slowly closer to becoming our most authentic, most confident selves.

Cuddy's work is thorough, passionate, and accessible to anyone. Cuddy shares her own personal experiences as well as numerous stories of individuals – everyday people from all walks of life and all areas of the globe – who have learned to approach the most challenging situations in life with confidence instead of fear, emerging victorious and satisfied.

AUTHOR'S STYLE

Perhaps the best word to summarize Cuddy's style in *Presence* is "real." Cuddy shares many of her personal experiences with her readers, bringing her concepts to us in a manner that is thorough, accessible, and practical. While the concepts she presents are serious, complex, and maybe even at times profound, Cuddy consistently delivers them in a manner that is open, honest, clear, and concise. Reading *Presence* feels very much like sitting with Cuddy and listening to her story, as well as the stories of others who have in turn been inspired by her.

While the book details numerous studies, experiments, and complex ideas, Cuddy puts them in terms that are easy-to-understand for the average reader as well as the more advanced. She shares just enough scientific detail to keep the most inquisitive of scholars intrigued while at the same time not so much that the rest of us are left behind. Cuddy's warm and caring personality shines through every word of her book ensuring that her material never feels intimidating, only inspiring.

AUTHOR'S PERSPECTIVE

Cuddy's perspective is a personal one. In addition to her research and numerous stories of people who have successfully implemented the theories that have evolved from her research, Cuddy has put her own research into practice, has "faked it till she made it," and nudged herself slowly but ever surely from a devastating brain injury to a career as a successful social psychologist and Harvard professor.

Cuddy's own story is touching and inspiring and she shares details of some very personal moments in her journey. By providing not only the perspective and testimony of other people but also herself, Cuddy makes her presentation that much more personal and accessible. Cuddy shows us how to connect with our truest, most authentic, and best selves by sharing with us how she was able to achieve the same in her own personal experience.

CHAPTER SUMMARIES

INTRODUCTION

Cuddy begins her introduction with anecdotes of people, all unique and memorable, who heard her 2012 TED talk on body language and presence and have approached her to say what a difference hearing her talk made in their lives. She briefly introduces the concepts she discusses in her book such as the idea of presence, the fake it till you become it concept, and the Wonder Woman in the bathroom idea.

In flashback, Cuddy tells the story of her brain injury at nineteen years of age. Cuddy and two college friends took a road trip from Missoula, Montana to Boulder, Colorado, dividing the trip into three shifts. During the shift when it was her turn to sleep, the driver lost control of the car and flipped it. Cuddy was thrown from the car and suffered a devastating diffuse axonal brain injury.

As a result of her injury, Cuddy's IQ dropped thirty points. She had to withdraw from college and subsequently received various treatments including occupational therapy, cognitive therapy, speech therapy, physical therapy, and psychological counseling. Six months after the injury, some of her closest friends observed that she was "just not the same anymore." Cuddy experienced confusion, anxiety, and frustration.

After a year, Cuddy returned to school but struggled to complete her work and had to drop out again. She recalls how people said things suggesting how lucky she was that she hadn't broken her neck, but Cuddy explains that people rarely think about the type of injuries that would cause unseen injury, such as that of the brain, which can very often cause drastic changes to our thinking, intellect, and personality.

Eventually, after a great deal of hard work and determination, Cuddy completed college four years after her pre-accident classmates and, as a result of her injury, entered the field of psychology. Her studies and her TED talk made her realize just how universal the desire for presence is among people from all walks of life and in every corner of the world.

Takeaways

- Cuddy's brain injury led her to the study of psychology and the science of presence.

- The opposite of powerlessness is not necessarily power. The best counteractive quality for powerlessness is presence. Presence gives us the power to rise to the challenging moments in life.

- Presence is a quality that stems from a belief and trust in yourself including your feelings, values, and abilities.

Highlights

- "Powerlessness engulfs us – and all that we believe, know, and feel. It enshrouds who we are, making us invisible. It even alienates us from ourselves."

- "Presence stems from believing in and trusting yourself – your real, honest feelings, values, and abilities. That's important, because if you don't trust yourself, how can others trust you?

CHAPTER 1 — WHAT IS PRESENCE?

In 2004, Cuddy attended a conference at which PhD candidates have an opportunity to present an encapsulated 90-second pitch of their PhD studies and goals to important people in the world of psychology. Cuddy found herself in an elevator with three well-established figures in the field and, when asked for her pitch, was unable to effectively deliver it, even though she knew her material inside out.

The phenomenon of realizing what one should or might have said only after the fact is referred to as "spirit of the stairs," a term coined by eighteenth century French philosopher Denis Diderot after losing a debate and realizing what his argument should have been only after leaving the gathering and reaching the foot of the stairs on his way out of the building.

This is something commonly experienced by many people during job interviews, auditions, when asking for a date, speaking aloud in a meeting or a class, and other challenging, high-stress situations. As long as you remain focused on the situation at hand, you will not be able to present the truest version of yourself. Cuddy recommends approaching these tense moments with confidence and excitement, imagining a successful outcome.

The Elements of Presence

At a department meeting, Cuddy had a realization that piqued her interest in the study of presence. A student was giving feedback about data she collected regarding the way entrepreneurs make pitches to potential investors and the investors' responses. The results were surprising: The strongest predictors of who got the money were not credentials or pitch, but rather traits of confidence, comfort level, and passionate enthusiasm. Did these findings really suggest that major decisions are based solely on *impressions* of the person giving the pitch?

Cuddy's reaction was that these qualities were signals of how much the person giving the pitch truly believed in the value and integrity of the idea and her ability to bring it to fruition. Are we correct to place so much value on this trait of enthusiastic confidence or is it superficial? The success of decisions such as these suggests that confidence is indeed a valid indicator of success.

We place our faith in people who project passion, confidence, and enthusiasm because these traits cannot easily be faked. When we try to fake our confidence or enthusiasm, others can tell something is off, even if they can't specifically identify what that something might be.

Presence is the Next Five Minutes

Cuddy has often asked the question "How do you define presence?" and has received answers from people all over the world. The differences and similarities in the answers are striking. Cuddy defines presence, as she uses the term in the book, to refer to a state of being attuned to and comfortable with our true thoughts, feelings, values, and potential. She stresses that it is not a permanent state of being, but rather something that comes and goes. Presence comes from a personal feeling of power, which allows us to be attuned to that true self.

What does Presence Look and Feel Like?

Presence manifests in two ways: First, when present, we communicate traits of passion, confidence, and comfortable enthusiasm. Second, presence comes through in something called *synchrony*.

Cuddy summarizes observations collected from successful venture capitalists over a period of years:

If they aren't buying what they're selling, neither is the customer. Presence comes from believing and trusting in yourself and your story. People cannot truly sell something if they don't believe in it and you can't sell a skill set you don't have. Presence doesn't mean pretending to be competent; it means eliminating whatever is blocking your ability to express what you're really about.

They try too hard to make a good impression and not showing enough that they care about the idea they're pitching. If we try to manage the impression we give others, we're presenting ourselves in an unnatural way and the result is that we come across as fake. But people still try to do this but does it really work? Research shows that the more people try to manage the impression they present, the more people see them as insincere and manipulative. Focus less on the impression you're making on others and more on the one you make on yourself.

They're too energetic, aggressive, and pushy and it seems defensive. Confidence and cockiness are often confused. Self-esteem and self-confidence are not synonymous, although they do share certain features. Truly confident people are not arrogant, which is simply a cover for insecurity. Truly confident people are grounded and believe in themselves and their ideas.

A little nervous is OK if you're doing something big that matters. Nervousness and anxiety interfere with concentration and focus, but can also keep us on our toes and help us avoid danger. It can sometimes signal respect. Trying to eliminate all evidence of nervousness is not necessary. Presence is confidence without arrogance.

Synchronous Self

Presence comes from an alignment (or synchrony) of the various elements of the self. In order to be present, elements of the self must work in harmony – emotions, thoughts, physical and facial expressions, and behaviors. Studies show that humans do not need verbal language to read one another. There is strong evidence that at least nine emotions are universal: anger, fear, disgust, happiness, sadness, surprise, contempt, shame, and pride. Our body language communicates these emotions.

Another way o define synchrony is to look at what *asynchrony* looks like. When people are inauthentic and not acting according to their true selves, nonverbal and verbal behaviors are misaligned and not in harmony. While being inauthentic is not the same as intentionally deceiving another person, the results are similar – we come across as not trustworthy.

Takeaways

- Presence comes and goes; it is a moment-to-moment experience, rather than something permanent in nature.

- Presence emerges when we feel powerful, allowing us to be attuned to our truest selves. Presence comes from within.

- Presence comes from an alignment, a synchronicity of the various elements of self. When the elements of our person are in harmony, we will be most able to convey our true selves.

Highlights

- "We can't be fully engaged in an interaction when we're busy second-guessing ourselves sand attending to the hamster wheel in our heads—the jumbled, frenetic, self-doubting analysis of what we *think* is happening in the room. ... Exactly when we most need to be present, we are least likely to be."

- "Presence, as I mean it throughout these pages, is the state of being attuned to and able to comfortably express our true thoughts, feelings, values, and potential."

- "What I'm saying here is that first impressions based on the qualities of enthusiasm, passion, and confidence *might* actually be quite sound—precisely because they're so hard to fake. When you are not present, people can tell. When you are, people respond. "

- "Sometimes you have to get out of the *way* of yourself so you can *be* yourself."

CHAPTER 2 — BELIEVING AND OWNING YOUR STORY

The self (as it relates to presence) is:

Multifaceted, not singular.

Expressed and reflected through our thoughts, feelings, values, and behaviors.

Dynamic and flexible, not static and rigid.

Cuddy believes the authentic self is a state of being that comes and goes, not a trait. It is the experience of *knowing* and *feeling* that you are being your bravest, truest self and expressing values through your actions. Our views of self are dependent upon the situations and contexts in which we find ourselves (parent, child, teacher, spouse, etc.). Being true to the self means the specifics of self change dependent upon the scenario.

Cuddy addresses the question of authentic *best* self versus authentic *true* self. There are parts of ourselves that we may dislike or even consider destructive and so we work to modify them. There are parts of ourselves that we also keep private. There are also parts of ourselves that are not destructive but we change or hide because we are ashamed of them. While we do not always choose to include these parts of ourselves in our ideal selves, they do represent a dimension of our authentic selves. All of our live experiences shape who we are so we may as well accept and own them.

Use these questions to identify the best parts of yourself:

- What three words best describe you as an individual?

- What unique qualities lead to your best performance and happiest times?

- When were you acting in a way that felt "right" and "natural" (at work or home)? Can you repeat that behavior today?

- What are your signature strengths and how can you use them?

But more than just identifying values, traits, and strengths of your authentic best self, you must also affirm and trust the answers; you must believe them. If you don't believe your entire personal story, neither will anyone else.

We see challenges in life as threats to our story or the adequacy of the person the story is about. Moments that threaten our sense of self tend to be those that are rooted in feelings of disapproval and rejection, such as not being admitted to a school, losing a job, ending a relationship, and more. Our instinct is to focus on the threat and defend ourselves. By affirming our most important values – the best parts of ourselves – before entering these threatening situations, we can attempt to defeat these potential threats before they even exist, leading to greater success in the actual scenarios we fear. This self-affirmation process is not about using generic pep-talk style mantras, but about defining and reinforcing your true self and trusting in your story.

In addition, *how* you self-affirm and tell your story matters just as much. Researchers who interviewed people in their 50s and 60s, a period of life marked by transitions in many areas of our lives, found that people who told their stories in a positive state of change experience significantly more positive mental health in following years than the people who described their stories in terms of negative change and outcomes.

Expressing Your Authentic Best Self

Once determining your authentic best self, you must determine how to express it as well. In order to be truly present, you have to not only know who you are and express that to others, but you also need to act upon that knowledge. In one study, a group of workers were asked to begin a set of tasks by first thinking about their individual selves. When they did, workers felt more connected to who they were and experienced more satisfaction from completing the tasks and performed better and with fewer errors. In organizations where employees were encouraged to express their true selves and individuality prior to company training performed jobs better and stayed at their jobs longer than employees training in groups that did not.

"Acting" with Presence

It is not possible to be present if you have not prepared in advance for what you have to do or say in any situation or performance. But eventually, you have to stop preparing *content* and begin to prepare a *mind-set*. To be present requires making a shift from what to say into how to say.

Takeaways

- The self is multifaceted, expressed through our thoughts and actions, and dynamic. It is a state, rather than a trait.
- Discover your authentic best self, then trust and believe that identity as an important part of your story.
- How you tell your story matters just as much as what your story is.

- To be present, you need to act upon who you are. AT some point you have to stop preparing content and actually prepare execution.

Highlights

- "To be present, it's not enough to know who you are and express it to others; you need to act on it."

- "By finding, believing, expressing, and then engaging our authentic best selves, especially if we do it right before our biggest challenges, we reduce our anxiety about social rejection and increase our openness to others. And that allows us to be fully present."

- "At some point, you must stop preparing content and start preparing mind-set. You have to shift from what you'll say to how you'll say it."

CHAPTER 3 – STOP PREACHING, START LISTENING: HOW PRESENCE BEGETS PRESENCE

Cuddy uses the story of a Boston minister who realized that a different solution was needed to address the problem of gang-related violence in the community around his church. What he and other clerics were doing until that point was accomplishing nothing; the minister realized that something different had to happen to bring about change. He realized that he had to be present - to actually show up - in order to make a difference.

Showing Up

The Boston ministers realized some key ideas. Presence with other is first about showing up, literally and physically. But after that, presence with others is about *how* we show up and how we approach the people we are hoping to influence. The

Boston ministers had to take an approach that was opposite any which had been tried with the youths before.

Research indicates that when we meet a new person, we quickly formulate answers to two questions: First, "Can I trust this person?" addresses the dimension of *warmth*. Second, "Can I respect this person?" addresses the dimension of *competence.*

But these traits are not valued equally. We judge warmth or trustworthiness first (and consider to be more important) because it is crucial to survival to determine whether a person is trustworthy. If not, that person is potentially dangerous. Competence is also valuable, but only after trustworthiness is determined.

The youth in the Boston example observed the ministers to determine two things. First, that they would be consistent not exploit the youth on the streets. After determining trust, the youth sought to evaluate strength. Could the ministers handle what was out there on the streets?

In Cuddy's research, she asks people if they would prefer to be seen as trustworthy or competent, and most choose competent. Competence is measurable in tangible, practical ways such as test scores, resume details, etc. While trustworthiness and warmth benefits other people, we believe that competence and strength benefit ourselves. In short, we prefer other people to be warm and trustworthy, but want to be seen by them as competent and strong.

Trust is a means of gaining influence and can only be achieved by being present. Cuddy ends this section with hope that readers will realize that finding presence in challenging moments is not only good for the individual, but can benefit others as well. Presence yields power to help others with *their* challenges

Stop Being Silk

The minister in Boston had to be real and true with the street youth. He had to make his real story clear, not the story he wanted people to believe. He had to be sincere in order to let them know it was safe for them to do the same.

Shutting Up

It is difficult for us to shut up and listen because when we meet someone, we fear they will not take us seriously and view us as "less than." We talk first in order to take charge, prove our worth, and demonstrate that we are in control. But by listening instead of talking first, we relinquish control and allow the other person to set the agenda – and that is a scary prospect.

Listening is crucial to presence, but real listening cannot happen without a sincere desire to hear and understand. In order to do this, we must give others the space and safety to be real and honest and not respond defensively.

There is a paradox of listening: by relinquishing power, we become more powerful. Several things happen when you stop talking and start listening:

- People can trust you.
- You acquire useful information.
- You begin to see other people as individuals – and maybe even allies.

- You develop solutions that other people are willing to accept and even adopt.

- When people feel heard, they are more willing to listen.

But none of this guarantees that listening to another person will result in a favorable outcome. Part of presence is accepting disappointment and remaining on course. What appears to be failure may eventually end up being an opportunity.

Letting Presence Speak for Itself

In a challenging situation, we sometimes express ourselves best by not expressing anything and simply allowing physical presence to speak for itself. Sometimes the act of just "being there" speaks volumes.

Takeaways

- Presence with others is first and foremost about showing up literally and physically. *How* we show up and approach people is also important.

- It is difficult to "shut up and listen" because when meeting someone for the first time, we fear not being taken seriously. We talk first to own the moment and assert our worth.

- Revealing your true self frees others to reveal their true selves.

- Listening is crucial to presence and true listening cannot happen unless we possess a sincere desire to hear and understand.

Highlights

- "The lesson is that trust is the conduit of influence, and the only way to establish real trust is by being present. Presence is the medium through which trust develops and ideas travel."

- "I'm also hoping to show you that learning to find presence in the most challenging moments isn't only good for you, it can yield great benefits for others as well. Presence gives you the power to help other in *their* most challenging moments."

- "What appears at first to be failure may actually be something else altogether – an opportunity to grow in an unanticipated way."

Chapter 4 – I Don't Deserve to Be Here

Cuddy shares the story of Pauline Rose Clance who, as a doctoral student in psychology, became convinced that she wasn't good enough to succeed. Clance believed everyone else was smarter than she was, that she got lucky, and that eventually she would fail. This thinking affected her life in many areas.

Clance's fear is one common to many of us – that somehow we've fooled people into believing we are more competent than we are. These fears go beyond simple performance anxiety; they cause deep, paralyzing belief that we are undeserving of any success and are doomed to fail. Psychologists refer to this as *impostor syndrome*.

It is not possible to be present if we feel like a fraud. Impostorism causes us to fixate on how we *think* others are judging us (and we're usually wrong), and then fixate further on how those judgments will affect our efforts. Impostorism steals power and stifles presence. Presence and impostorism are on opposing sides of our selves.

Feeling Like an Imposter

Despite her doubts, Clance succeeded in gaining a faculty position at Oberlin College. While there she taught and worked in the counseling center. She realized that these feelings of impostorism and uncertainty were prevalent among high-performing females, that despite any external achievements, they feared their accomplishments were attributable to luck rather than actual skill.

Clance and collaborator Suzanne Imes investigated what they called the impostor phenomenon (IP), defined as "an internal experience of intellectual phoniness" in which women fear having what they believe are their true abilities (or lack of abilities) exposed.

Clance worked with Nancy Zumoff to develop a scale to measure the extent to which a person did or did not feel this way, asking subjects to rate a series of statements as true or false. Sample statements follow:

- I'm afraid people important to me may find out that I'm not as capable as they think I am.

- Sometimes I feel or believe that my success in life or in my job has been the result of some kind of error.

- When I've succeeded at something and received recognition for my accomplishments, I have doubts that I can keep repeating that success.

- I often compare my ability to those around me and think they may be more intelligent than I am.

- If I receive a great deal of praise and recognition for something I've accomplished I tend to discount the importance of what I've done.

Clance and Imes published the first academic paper on IP, which focused on the experiences of women who seemed to suffer from it and treatments for it as a mental health issue.

This Is Much Bigger Than We Thought...

Eventually, Clance and others studying impostorism realized it was much more far-reaching than they knew. Men and women both experienced impostorism to an equal degree. But if that was true, why did it appear to be a women's problem?

First, some people have trouble recognizing it in themselves. Another likely possibility was that men do not as readily talk about this type of problem, perhaps from fear of "stereotype backlash," harassment, or ostracism for failing to conform to societal expectations. This can happen to anyone, though, not only men. So while men and women both experience impostorism, men may be more burdened by it because they do not share it as openly as women.

In addition to crossing gender lines, impostorism is something that nearly everyone experiences at some point in their lives and does not exclude by gender, race, culture, or any other demographic characteristic. Even though it is a widespread experience, it is impossible to determine the cause of impostorism. There are many factors that affect the appearance of impostorism and so it cannot be linked to any one particular cause.

Trapped by the Impostor

Cuddy cites more examples of obviously successful people who have admitted struggles with impostorism – author Neil Gaiman and a woman named Elena who earned a PhD in physics from one of the most rigorous science programs in the world, for example. When we feel like impostors, we can't assign our success to something internal and constant to our nature such as talent or ability. Rather, we credit our success to outside forces such as luck.

Research has identified self-defeating behaviors of "impostors." For example, they expect to do badly on exams, even with a record of performing well, and they overestimate the number of mistakes made when the exam is finished. Behaviors like these reinforce our beliefs that we are not as good as the world perceives us to be and wend up relentlessly criticizing ourselves, paving a path to failure for ourselves. Research shows that focusing on possible outcomes of performance in high-pressure situations will measurably diminish skills.

I Was an Impostor Myself

Cuddy outlines her own experiences with impostorism, discussing once again her experiences as she made the journey back after her brain injury, her desire to quit, and her fight to continue until she finally realized that she could succeed. Ultimately, she realized that she was *not* a fraud and *did* deserve credit for her successes. She discusses the effect her TED talk had on her audience and her surprise that it resonated with so many people.

Can We Break Up with Our Impostor Selves?

Cuddy concludes this chapter with some insights about moving past our feelings of imposterism. Most people experience these feelings, but few talk about it openly. If we all knew how many others feel the same, we would arrive at the conclusion that either we are *all* impostors or our personal assessments are inaccurate. The feelings of inadequacy and isolation that impostorism produces serve only to further discourage us. Most people will probably never shed impostor fears completely, but rather will continue to work out those fears one at a time. By becoming aware of our insecurities and opening up about them, we become better able to deal with them.

Takeaways

- The feeling that we don't belong and have fooled people into thinking we are more competent than we truly are is common. Psychologists refer to this feeling as *impostor syndrome* or *impostorism.*

- We cannot be truly present when we feel like a fraud. Impostorism causes over thinking and second-guessing, making us fixate on how we imagine others judge us. Presence and impostorism are opposing sides of the same coin – and we are the coin.

- People who have achieved something and are demonstrably anything *but* frauds fear failure most.

Impostorism detracts from our ability to feel confident about what we do well.

- Research shows that focusing on possible outcomes of performance in high-pressure situations will measurably diminish skills.

Highlights

- "Impostorism steals our power and suffocates our presence. If even *you* don't believe you should be here, how will you convince anybody else?"

- "The imposter experience stops us from reacting in the moment – it keeps us from responding to the world as it truly exists."

- "...the more we are aware of our anxieties, the more we communicate about them, and the smarter we are about how they operate, the easier they'll be to shrug off ht next time they pop up."

CHAPTER 5 — HOW POWERLESSNESS SHACKLES THE SELF (AND HOW POWER SETS IT FREE)

While the details of people's personal stories of powerlessness differ, the basic premise is similar: change accompanies a perception of loss of power and strength, followed by feelings of insecurity, anxiety, discouragement, and defeat. Physical manifestations of powerlessness also follow along with a loss of confidence and ambition.

Social psychologist Dacher Keltner explains this cycle: Power activates a psychological and behavioral *approach system*. Feelings of power yield feelings of freedom, control, and safety. We then become more sensitive to opportunities than to threats, feel positive and optimistic, and feel unrestricted by social pressure. Powerlessness, however, activates a psychological and behavioral *inhibition system*. We become more sensitive to threats than to opportunities, feel generally anxious and pessimistic, and feel inhibited by social pressures.

In decision making, we focus on one of two things: either the potential benefits or the potential costs of the action. Focusing on the potential benefits makes us more likely to take action; focusing on the potential costs makes us less likely to act and thus avoid potential dangers.

Power affects many aspects of our selves in ways that directly facilitate or obstruct our presence and performance. It is not possible to be present when we feel powerless.

Personal Power versus Social Power

Social power is the ability to exert dominance and influence control over others' behavior. Personal power is characterized by freedom *from* the dominance of others. Social power is our ability to influence others' behavior (power *over* others). Personal power is freedom *from* the dominance of others (power *to* control our own states and behaviors). It is most desirable to achieve both kinds of power but personal power is particularly important. We cannot achieve presence through social power unless we have first achieved personal power.

Feeling powerlessness prevents us from trusting in ourselves and, as a result, failing to build trust with others. In a perfect world, personal power would be unfailing. In reality, however, it is likely to fluctuate, especially when we experience difficulty in life. Whether or not we feel powerful or powerless ultimately has consequences for our lives.

The Paradox of Powerlessness

Threats exist for all people, but feelings of powerlessness increase our perception of potential danger and set off a chain reaction that disables us even more. An increase sense of danger increases social anxiety in several ways:

Feeling Powerless Impairs Thought

When feelings of powerlessness take hold, clear-thinking is lost and our brains cannot meet the demands of stressful situations. Powerlessness undermines executive function –

higher-order tools such as reasoning, task flexibility, and attention control which are all necessary to cope with challenging situations. Without proper executive functioning, powerlessness blocks our abilities and makes it difficult to show our true selves.

Powerlessness Makes Us Self-Absorbed

Anxiety alienates us from others and interferes with the ability to see the world from others' perspective. Anxiety and self-absorption share a bi-directional link – they cause each other. Anxiety causes something called the spotlight effect – the sense that people are paying more attention to us than is actually true and most often in a negative way rather than positive. This self-absorption does not stem from ego or narcissism, but rather from the belief that each of us is, simply, the center of our own universe. We see the world from our own perspective and expect that others do as well.

Powerlessness Prevents Presence

Anxiety and self-absorption during a challenging situation can cause us to spend time *post-event processing* – continuing to think about and replay a situation even days later. Essentially, our memory is warped and full of holes. Anxiety makes it nearly impossible to be present before, during, and after a challenging situation.

The Benefits of Feeling Powerful

Feeling powerless inhibits and depletes us; feeling powerful does the opposite.

Power Can Protect Us

Research indicates that power serves as a buffer against negative emotions. It allows us to develop a "thick skin" against judgments, rejection, stress, and pain. Even hypothetical power can produce these effects.

Power Can Connect Us

Feelings of power can improve our ability to read and relate to other people. People who feel powerful tend to make better judgments of emotional expression and tend to be more forgiving of others.

Power Can Liberate Our Thinking

A lack of power impairs cognitive function but having power may enhance it, improving our decision-making ability, especially in difficult situations. Power makes us fearless, independent, and less susceptible to outside pressures. Power allows us to be more creative.

Power Can Synchronize Us

Feelings of power help synchronize our thoughts, feelings, and behaviors, thus bringing us closer to true presence.

Power Can Incite Action

Power causes people to act. Research indicates that feelings of power make people more proactive, giving us freedom to decide, to act, and do to. Similarly, powerlessness can lead to inaction and being dependent upon others who are more powerful to provide examples for our own behavior.

Power Can Make Our Actions More Effective

Power affects performance in high-stress situations whereas powerlessness inhibits performance. When we feel powerful, we are inspired. Feelings of power can change our perception of emotions during high-stress scenarios and increase feelings of self-confidence. People who *believe* they are able to do something are more likely to *actually* do it.

Power Affects Our Physiology

To this point in the book, Cuddy's discussion of her research on power has focused on the cognitive and emotional elements of power and powerlessness. Now Cuddy raises the question of whether power is all in our heads. Cuddy says no: power is not just a state of mind; it is a force of nature and has a physical aspect. The research to back these statements is detailed in the section that follows.

Does Power Corrupt?

Power helps us fixate less on other people's perceptions of us, but can also cause us to think less about other people. In short, power has the ability to either corrupt or reveal. Cuddy's hope is that personal power (because it is infinite and does not require control of another person) can be perceived as abundant, something we can share. Cuddy believes that personal power has the potential to be contagious – the more personally powerful we feel, the more we will want to help others feel the same way. Power reveals, bringing us closer to our best and truest selves, while a lack of power distorts and obscures.

Cuddy ends with the idea that if power reveals, then we can only know others who are truly powerful because only they have the ability and courage to show their true selves to others.

Takeaways

- Power makes us approach; powerlessness makes us avoid. When we feel powerless, we cannot be present.
- Social power is power *over* – the capacity to control others' states and behaviors. Personal power is power *to* – the ability to control our own states and behaviors.

- Ideally, people would possess both kinds of power, but personal power is most essential to discovering our true selves.

- Powerlessness is at least as likely to corrupt as power is. Power can corrupt and also reveal.

Highlights

- "Power affects our thoughts, feelings, behaviors, and even physiology in fundamental ways that directly facilitate or obstruct our presence, our performance, and the very course of our lives."

- "Unless and until we feel personally powerful, we cannot achieve presence, and all the social power in the world won't compensate for its absence."

- "The feeling that arises from personal power is not the desire to have control; it's the effortless feeling of being in control – lucid, calm, and not dependent on the behavior of others."

CHAPTER 6 — SLOUCHING, STEEPLING, AND THE LANGUAGE OF THE BODY

Power Expands Our Body Language

Power expands our bodies as well as our minds. Expansive and open body language is tied to dominance across the animal kingdom. Simply expressed, feelings of power cause us to make ourselves bigger (wider stance, outspread arms, full chest). Status and power are expressed through expansive, nonverbal displays.

Nonverbal behavior operates through channels such as facial expressions, eye movements and gaze, body orientation and posture, hand gesture, walking style, vocal cues, and more. Even gestures with the hands or fingers can signal power, such as "steepling" which may be subtle, but is still spatially expansive. Power also affects how we perceive stature – both in ourselves and others. For example, when we are confident and feel powerful, we perceive ourselves as taller and others as smaller than they actually are.

Cuddy cites research and evidence to address the questions of whether nonverbal behaviors are learned or hardwired – are they nurture or nature? She cites studies conducted by Charles Darwin that proposed expressions of emotion are biologically innate and evolutionarily adaptive, that they signal important social information. Expressions of emotion serve us by prompting immediate action that benefits us depending upon environmental circumstances. Darwin suggested certain emotional expressions are universal.

More complex signals of power or powerlessness may also be universal. Cuddy discusses evidence from studies done by Jessica Tracy who has extensively studied the emotion of pride, which arises from feelings of power, strength, and victory. Tracy's studies suggest, like Darwin's, that these expressions of pride are an evolved part of us as humans and also universal. Consider the spontaneous expressions of pride used by athletes from all over the world, for example. Athletes tend to show the same behaviors after winning (such as smiling, head tilted back, arms raised, chest out) or losing (shoulders slumped, chin down, chest narrowed).

These victory expressions serve a purpose. Tracy's research suggests they have evolved to produce physiological changes (such as increasing testosterone) that would allow us to continue to dominate or defend. They may also have evolved as a social function, communicating status or power.

Walking and Talking with a Swagger

Aside from postures and gestures, consider the question of bodies in motion. Do feelings of power cause us to move in certain ways? Cuddy's team worked with Nikolaus Troje to determine the relationships between movement of the body and various emotions such as happiness, sadness, relaxation, and anxiety. Cuddy discusses the process and details of the study. When we feel powerful, we tend to walk and speak in more expansive ways such as swinging our arms or taking a longer stride, initiating conversation, speaking more slowly, and making eye contact.

Powerlessness Collapses Your Body

On the flip side, powerlessness not only constrains our thoughts, feelings, and actions, but also our bodies. When we feel powerless or subordinate, we constrict posture by tightening and making ourselves smaller by slumping, lowering our head, or slouching in posture. We also use gestures that restrict speech such as hesitating, rushing, using small range or higher pitch. Powerlessness also inhibits facial expressions. When we feel uncomfortable, insecure, or unsafe, we signal fear to protect ourselves from potential predators. In short, when we feel powerless in any way, we make ourselves smaller. This in turns causes other people to see us as powerless and frightened.

Body Language and Gender

In general, men display more nonverbal dominance and expansiveness, talk more, and interrupt more than women. Women generally behave in more submissive, contractive nonverbal behavior, talk less, and interrupt less often (and are interrupted more). Men and women also seem to walk differently. Culture affects these various differences as well. Cuddy and her colleagues conducted studies of young children and their responses to powerful and expansive behaviors. Even young children associate powerful poses with males and powerless poses with females.

Should We Just Dominate Everybody with Our Body Language?

Powerful body language signals others to either approach or avoid us. But poses typically used in evolutionarily adaptive scenarios are not particularly useful in contemporary scenarios such as meetings, classrooms, or family discussion. Intentionally using such power cues can backfire when we intentionally use them for effect. There are several reasons trying to use high-power nonverbal expression to influence others is a bad idea:

Intimacy, Not Intimidation

Status and power are not synonymous, but they are closely related. Research indicates we pay more attention to high-status, dominant individuals. Dominant members of a group tend to influence decisions set norms, incite conflict, and resolve disputes.

Studies Cuddy and a team of colleagues conducted on gaze aversion indicate that people do not want to engage with others who are intentionally displaying dominance. Their behavior is perceived as dangerous. Humans are turned off by excessive eye contact, perceiving it as a blatant and arrogant attempt to dominate. The best case scenario is to work toward intimacy, not intimidation.

You Might Be Violating Cultural Norms

Body language norms vary among cultures and it is important to understand them, particularly in cross-cultural interactions. Cultural misunderstandings about body langue can make or break potentially lucrative deals. If we do not take the time to understand these differences, it can result in lost job opportunities, lost business deals, and more.

Thoughts and feelings shape body language and body language speaks to other people. We use our nonverbal communication to hold entire conversations without ever saying a word. But body language also speaks to our inner selves.

Takeaways

- Power expands our minds as well as our bodies; powerlessness collapses our minds and bodies. Power also affects our perception of our own stature as well as the stature of others.

- There are many channels for communicating nonverbal messages – facial expressions, eye movements and gaze, body orientation and posture, hand gestures, waling style, vocal cues (pitch, volume), and more. Many of these messages and emotions are universal.

- Although nonverbal communication of power messages is universal, gender and culture play a role in the type of behavior exhibited.

Highlights

- "Whether temporary or stable, benevolent or sinister, status and power arc expressed through evolve nonverbal displays – widespread limbs, enlargement of occupied space, erect posture."

- "Let's stop thinking about powerful postures as masculine and powerless postures as feminine. I'm not advocating that you sit with your knees wide apart or your feet up on the desk while in a meeting or that you engage in alpha body language in your interactions – whether you are a man or a woman. I'm telling you that you *deserve* to adopt open, comfortable postures and to take up your fair share of space regardless of your gender."

- "Well, it's clear that thoughts and feelings shape body langue and that each person's body language speaks to others. Using a purely physical vocabulary, our inner lives communicate, person to person, back and forth. We're holding entire conversations, exchanging important information, without ever saying a word."

CHAPTER 7 – SURFING, SMILING, AND SINGING OURSELVES TO HAPPINESS

Journalist Eve Fairbanks compares learning to surf to learning how to live on land. Learning to surf is a task that captures the mind-body connection, how it works, and why we overlook it. We focus too much on skills we think we need rather than deciding to perform the action. Rather than decisions coming *from* confidence, Fairbanks says, decisions *create* confidence.

"I'm Happy Because I Sing"

It is a myth that the body, brain, and mind are separate entities. The brain and the body are parts of a single integrated, complicated, and beautiful system. Psychologist William James (1842-1910) asserted "I don't sing because I'm happy; I'm happy because I sing." This idea indicates that bodily experiences cause emotions, rather than the converse.

We experience physical sensations with our bodies and that in turn causes certain feelings.

Believing that emotions are interpretations of bodily experiences, James believed we can fake emotion until we actualize it – in other words, fake it until we make it. We can sing ourselves into happiness or cry ourselves into despair. James also proved that an impaired mind-body connection results in a diminished ability to read emotional responses in others.

About Face

Studies show that facial expressions can affect our moods; sad expressions make us feel sad, happy expressions make us feel happy, and so on. Similarly to how performing certain facial expressions creates emotions, preventing or hindering facial expressions can block emotions.

Presence Through the Body

If facial expressions can impact emotions, is it also true that our bodily actions can make us feel powerful, confident, and more authentic? In other words, can physical actions lead to presence? Evidence suggests that where our bodies lead, our minds and emotions follow.

You Already Have the Tools You Need to Become Present

Studies of post-traumatic stress (PTS) indicate that there are psychological and physiological benefits to yoga – not only for people with PTS, but for anyone. People experience benefits after even one short chair-based yoga session. Participants in studies reported decreases in stress and breathing rates. The tools we need to become present are built right into our biology: one is breathing, an action so basic that we rarely even think about it. Controlling the way we breathe enables us to control our emotions and state of mind.

Posing Our Way to Presence

Our bodies communicate with us, telling us how or what to feel and think. How we carry ourselves (including facial expressions, posture, breathing) affects how we think, feel, and behave.

Takeaways

- The body and brain are part of an integrated, complicated, and beautiful system. When we experience physical sensations, we develop certain emotional responses.

- William James assertion "I don't sing because I'm happy; I 'm happy because I sing" suggests that it is possible to fake an emotion until we actualize it.

- The "idea of oneself" is a concept that suggests the self can be anything you want it to be, but that doesn't make it insincere or inauthentic. Instead, it suggests you can think of yourself in a particular manner and then take steps to make that self a reality.

Highlights

- "[Eve] Fairbanks believes that learning to surf taught her something about how to live on dry land." As she wrote in the *Washington Post,* 'Surfing distills into a pure physical moment the usually drawn-out, intellectual, complex challenge of simultaneously accepting what life throws at you and making the best of it.'"

- "Our bodies speak to us. They tell us how and what to feel and even think." They change what goes on inside our endocrine systems, our autonomic nervous systems, our brains, and our minds without our being conscious of a thing. How you carry yourself — your facial expressions, your postures, your breathing — all clearly affect the way you think, feel, and behave."

- "The tools we need to become present are built into our biology. One of them is an action so basic that we usually forget we're doing it: breathing."

CHAPTER 8 – THE BODY SHAPES THE MIND (SO STARFISH UP!)

Cuddy paid little attention to body language until after her accident. Being a passenger in a car became something terrifying. Instinctively, Cuddy would curl into a ball, shut down mentally. If she had pretended to be brave and forced her body to trick her mind into believing she was safe, would she have become less powerless and more present?

Fifteen years later, two experiences helped Cuddy make sense of the situation. Cuddy observed participating and non-participating students in a classroom. Non-participating students were in the room, but were absent. Meeting an FBI body-language expert and other experts in the field intimidated her. Cuddy let fear and nervousness prevent her from being present and act like the nonparticipating students, even though she wanted to participate more than anything.

The way we carry our bodies determines the path our lives will take and is a source of personal power that allows us to unlock our true selves. Expanding your body expands your mind and allows you to be present. Controlling body language is about more than posing in powerful ways. It is also about realizing that we pose in power*less* ways more often than we think.

Our Experiments in Power Posing

Cuddy's team developed an experiment to address the question of connection between emotions and physical expressions. If we naturally expand our bodies when feeling powerful, do we also then feel powerful when we expand our bodies? The team began by examining two factors: feelings of power and confidence and willingness to take risks.

Subjects were asked to adopt power poses or powerless poses. The results of their first studies provided evidence that adopting expansive, open postures caused psychological and behavioral changes as well as physiological changes. This paralleled the known effects of power. Carrying ourselves in powerful ways directs feelings, behaviors, and the body to feel more powerful and to be present in various situations.

Cuddy discusses in detail the specifics of various examples and studies that explain these theories. The most concise summary statements of these extended examples follow.

- **Feeling:** *Expanding your body language – through posture, movement, and speech – makes you feel more confident and powerful, less anxious and self-absorbed, and generally more positive.*

- **Thinking:** *Expanding your body causes you to think about yourself in a positive light and to trust in that self-concept. It also clears your head, making space for creativity, cognitive persistence, and abstract thinking.*

- **Acting:** *Expanding your body frees you to approach, act, and persist.*

- **Body:** *Expanding your body physiologically prepares you to be present; it overrides your instinct to fight or flee, allowing you to be grounded, open, and engaged.*

- **Pain:** *Expanding your body toughens you to physical pain.*

Performance and Presence

All of the effects of expansive body language facilitate our ability to achieve presence during challenges. These effects include increasing feelings of power, confidence, and optimism, decreasing feelings of stress, shoring up positivity of self-image, freeing us to be assertive, to take action, and to persist in the face of challenge, and preparing our bodies to be strong and grounded. High-power poses lead to higher nonverbal presence which is perceived by others.

iPosture

Studies also indicate that technology – phones, tablets, laptops – produces the same effect on people as powerless postures. Technology in and of itself makes it difficult to be present, but these devices additionally force us into physical positions that decrease power and presence. And the smaller the device, the more limiting the posture. The end result is a cruel irony: we spend hours each day working on small mobile devices with the goal of increasing productivity and efficiency, but using these small devices may actually reduce our assertiveness and potentially undermine productivity and efficiency.

Picturing Powerful Posture (Your Body's in Your Head)

Could imagining expansive behavior and power poses result in an increase of presence? Would it be possible to encourage people with physical disabilities, for example, to feel more powerful by imagining expansive postures?

Years of research has shown that mental imagery of movement or action closely imitates actual physical movement or action. Cuddy's research has indicated that it is not necessary to have a fully functioning physical body to benefit from power posing and expansive behaviors. Many people (whether physically disabled or not) find themselves in situations where space or privacy are not readily available to practice a power pose. But it is always possible to imagine these behaviors and reap similar benefits.

Virtual Posture

The benefits of power posing also carry over into virtual space. The physical characteristics of your avatar, for example, can affect the way you behave in real life. Research shows that when people perceptually inhabit virtual representations of themselves, they adopt the characteristics of their avatars. This is known as the "body transfer illusion."

Stand at Attention

Soldiers often "stand at attention" with chin up, chest out, shoulders, back, stomach in. It is an upright, grounded, motionless posture that signals respect and is also most conducive to feelings of alertness and strength. The reason behind this posture for soldiers is simple: when receiving information that could influence life-or-death decisions, soldiers must be fully psychologically present and standing at attention accomplishes this.

When we stop paying attention, we are more likely to experience the negative outcomes of both expansive *and* contractive posture. When we do not pay attention, we may perform less effectively or admirably. Studies and experiments indicate that being aware of and having control over our personal power are crucial to presence and "standing at attention" helps achieve this awareness and control.

Starfish Up!

Many people suffer from feelings of personal powerlessness and consent to them, which results in reinforcing these feelings and blocking our path forward. We can use our bodies to gain personal power. Adopting a starfish or Wonder Woman pose will not be effective for every person in every situation, but the idea is that no matter the technique, there are numerous ways to practice expansive posture. Find the techniques that work for you. Expanding your body will bring you to the present and improve your performance. Body language affects how others perceive us and how we perceive ourselves. The way you carry yourself shapes the way you carry out your life.

Takeaways

Expanding your body expands your mind. That enables you to be more present, which has far-reaching results. Taking control of body language is about posing in powerful ways and also about recognizing that we pose in powerless ways more often than we think, leading to negative effects.

Carrying ourselves in powerful ways directs our feelings, thoughts, behaviors, and physical body to feel more powerful, be more present, and perhaps perform better in various situations.

Many people experience circumstances where we are unable to physically power pose before facing a big challenge. But we can always imagine ourselves practicing an expansive posture in our mind and reap similar benefits.

Body language affects the way others perceive us and affects the way we perceive ourselves. The way we carry our bodies shapes the way we carry out our lives.

Highlights

"The way we carry ourselves form moment to moment blazes the trail our lives take. When we embody shame and powerlessness, we submit to the status quo, whatever that may be. We acquiesce to emotions, actions, and outcomes hat we resent. We don't share who we really are. And all this has real-life consequences.

"Perhaps the most important and robust finding is that, as we showed in our experiments, by adopting expansive, open postures, we make ourselves *feel* better and more effective in several ways. We feel more powerful, confident, and assertive, less stressed and anxious, and happier and more optimistic."

"How you carry your body shapes how you carry out your life. Your body shapes your mind. Your mind shapes your behavior. And your behavior shapes your future. Let your body tell you that you're powerful and deserving, and you become more present, enthusiastic, and authentically yourself. "

CHAPTER 9 – HOW TO POSE FOR PRESENCE

So when should we power pose? The possibilities are widely varied. The number of challenging situations is as great as the number of people experiencing them. While there is no concrete answer that applies to everyone, Cuddy shares some common scenarios collected from people who have used power poses successfully. Power poses can be helpful in the following scenarios (and so many more):

- entering new situations, meeting new people, learning or speaking a non-native language
- speaking up for yourself or for someone else
- requesting help
- ending a personal or professional relationship
- quitting a job
- giving or receiving critical feedback

No two people face the same challenges so it is important to understand the situations (and people) that trigger powerless body language in yourself so that you can make use of power posing when it is most useful to you.

Prepare with Big Poses

By taking up as much space as you comfortably can before a big challenge, you are telling yourself that you are powerful. This enables you to face the challenge as your boldest, most authentic self. It's a pre-event warm-up that optimizes your brain to be 100 percent present. Cuddy includes a list of examples including power posing first thing in the morning, posing in an elevator or bathroom stall during the day, and standing in waiting rooms rather than hunching over your phone.

Present with Good Posture

In addition to striking bold power poses *before* a challenging situation, it is also important to maintain strong, upright, and open postures *during* a challenging situation. Power poses don't exactly work in the middle of a presentation or meeting and power poses in the midst of actual interactions can backfire, as discussed in earlier chapters. But there are more subtle ways to maintain bold posture and, therefore, maintain presence. A list of suggestions includes keeping shoulders back and chest open, breathing slowly and deeply, and keeping feet grounded (no ankle-wrapping) so that you feel solid and balanced.

Mind Your Posture Throughout the Day

It is important to avoid mindlessly falling into powerless poses. Suggestions for doing this include setting posture reminders on your phone, organizing spaces where you spend your time in ways that encourage good posture, and combining power poses with daily routines such as keeping a hand on your hip while brushing your teeth.

Takeaways

- It is important to notice situations (and people) that trigger powerless body language in ourselves so that we know when to adopt power posing to counteract these situations in advance.

- Use power poses to speak to yourself before entering a big challenge. Taking up as must space as is comfortably possible tells your body that you're powerful and optimizes your brain to be 100 percent present.

- It is just as important to maintain strong, upright, and open postures during challenging situations as it is to use them before challenging situations.

Highlights

- "Most of us would benefit from a power boost before a job interview, a meeting with an authority figure, a class discussion, a difficult conversation, a negotiation, an audition, an athletic event, or a presentation before a group."

- "You'll also benefit enormously if you can get in the habit of checking in on your posture, both during challenging situations and generally throughout the day."

- "It's important to avoid falling into the powerless poses we often mindlessly inhabit."

Chapter 10 – SelfoNudging: How Tiny Tweaks Lead to Big Changes

Cuddy talks about how she used to panic under pressure and would jump into what she calls "make-it-better-by-doing-something-*anything*-mode." Eventually Cuddy realized that slowing down is a power move and that doing nothing is actually doing something.

In a challenging situation, we must nudge ourselves toward being more courageous, acting more boldly. We nudge ourselves toward being present. But we don't achieve these things by deciding to change *right now*. Rather, we do it in small increments.

Nudges

Studies indicate that the best way to change behavior for the better is to do so subtly, nudging people little by little toward change. The process may not be dramatic, but the changes that result are. Over time, these small nudges and changes build upon themselves and produce significant results.

- Nudges are effective for various reasons
- Nudges are small and require minimal psychological and physical commitment.
- Nudges operate via psychological shortcuts.

Our attitudes follow from our behaviors.

Self-nudges are minimal modifications to one's own body language and/or mid-set that are meant to produce small psychological and behavioral improvements in the moment. They have the potential to lead to big changes over time. When we self-nudge, the gap between reality and goal is narrow rather than daunting and we are less apt to quit. This results in changes that are more authentic and longer-lasting.

Incremental Change – Baby Steps

Carol Dweck and her team of collaborators have conducted studies that show children thrive in school when they adopt a growth mind-set (belief that they can improve in a given area) as opposed to a fixed mind-set (belief that their abilities cannot be changed). This idea extends beyond academic performance. Nudges are about building an environment in which people make good decisions. Nudging yourself allows you to be both builder *and* building, creating a space for positive, healthful behaviors.

How We Nudge Ourselves from Tiny Tweaks to Big Changes

Adjusting posture is the ultimate tiny tweak. In order to make the effects last, they need to be reinforced with opportunities to take root, grow, and fortify. Our behavior reinforces our behavior. We derive our attitudes from our behavior as opposed to behaving based on our attitudes. Self-nudges also produce lasting effects through other people's reinforcement of our behavior.

Why Many Popular Self-Change Approaches Fail – And Even Backfire

Why self-nudge instead of make a commitment to change, and then follow through? Big changes are too ambitious and focus on a goal that is dependent upon the success of many smaller changes. Big resolutions also focus on the negative things we want to eliminate rather than the positive things we want to encourage. This can be de-motivating. Finally, large resolutions undermine intrinsic motivation, the personal and internal desire to do something, by replacing it with external motivation. Extrinsic motivators won't always be present. More effective change comes from within.

Self-Nudges

Body-mind intervention is not the only way to self-nudge. Various small tweaks can be employed to strengthen psychological well-being, change behavior, and improve follow-through. Small nudges work well for anxiety. Reframing anxiety as excitement can produce great benefits. We often see ourselves as our own worst enemy. We need to like and respect ourselves as much as we would another person in order to nudge ourselves forward. Decrease gaps between your present self and your future self to help make a connection. Self-nudging can be as simple as clothing choice. What we ear can change how we see, feel, think, and behave.

Takeaways

- We don't achieve large goals or changes by deciding to change *right now*. We do it gently, incrementally, by nudging ourselves – a bit further every time.

- Incremental changes, based on tiny nudges, can lead to professional success, confidence, comfort, improved self-efficacy, better relationships, health, and well-being.

- For the effects of nudging to stick, they need opportunity to be reinforced.

Highlights

- "When you give yourself a self-nudge, the gap between reality and goal is narrow; it's not daunting, which means you're less likely to give up. As a result, your behavior change is more authentic, lasting, and self-reinforcing.

- Reframing an emotion, making friends with a picture of your future self, wearing clothing that fits the role – these are just a few of the ways in which we can change the future by slowly, incrementally changing how we interact with the present.

- "With each self-nudge, pleasure builds upon pleasure, power upon power, and presence upon presence."

CHAPTER 11 – FAKE IT TILL YOU BECOME IT

In the final chapter, Cuddy shares several stories from people who have been helped and inspired by her message on presence – people who achieved success by faking it until they became it. People are making use of Cuddy's techniques and finding success in all areas of life.

The ideal outcome of presence is to achieve a "comfortable confidence" and synchrony that enables us to face challenging situations and to emerge from them feeling a sense of satisfaction and accomplishment. Situations in which we feel the most challenged and where stakes are highest is where power and present matter most.

Cuddy reminds readers that her book is about being present in the moments that we find most challenging and about trusting that those moments will build upon themselves as we nudge forward. Ultimately, those moments can change our lines.

The most commonly quoted line from Cuddy's TED talk is "Don't' fake it till you make it, fake it till you become it." That is what Presence is about – slowly nudging yourself toward the best version of yourself, and being present during those challenging moments. Even if you don't feel it yet, do it anyway.

Takeaways

- The ideal benefit of present is to achieve a comfortable confidence that allows us to come away from challenging situations feeling satisfied and accomplished.

- Situations that involve the most challenge and the highest stakes are where power and presence matter the most.

- Presence is about nudging yourself slowly toward the best version of yourself possible.

Highlights

- "My hope is that you will recognize yourself somewhere among them. I say this because I believe that the part of my TED talk that had the biggest impact was not the research I presented, it was my confession that I've spent a good part of my life believing 'I don't deserve to be here.' Although I didn't understand it at the time, I now see why that mattered: it made people feel less alone in the world, knowing that at least one other person has felt this way and has (mostly) overcome that feeling. One true story, one honest confession, can be powerful."

- "Don't fake it till you make it, fake it till you become it."

- "Dance your way to presence. Seize the large, beautiful, powerful parts of yourself- the ones you love and believe. They are, indeed, yours for the taking."

CONCLUDING ANALYSIS

Amy Cuddy's *Presence* teaches readers how to access their truest, most authentic selves in order to achieve power and confidence. The book expands upon concepts presented in Cuddy's 2012 TED talk, one of the most-views TED talks to date.

Cuddy tells readers early in the book that while most talks such as hers emerge from books, her experience worked in reverse. As a result of the reaction to her talk and the number of people who approached her with stories of their success using her techniques, Cuddy realized it was necessary to share more information on the subject.

In many ways Cuddy's research and techniques may be considered ground-breaking. But at the same time, much of what is presented is simply good old-fashioned common sense. The concepts are not necessarily earth-shattering, but the steps she presents for how to go about accessing the skills and techniques in the book, coupled with real-life success stories from people all over the world provide support for the reliability of her ideals.

The simple, practical methods Cuddy shares that anyone can start using right now, today, to begin to move toward the comfortable confidence she describes make the book highly relatable. So while Cuddy's basic premises may not be earth-shattering, they are indeed potentially life-altering, providing readers with a tangible and usable plan for achieving happiness and success.

Overall, Amy Cuddy's *Presence* is an interesting and informative read. She combines warmth, wit, and intelligence to effortlessly present detailed scientific concepts in a practical and accessible format.

Made in the USA
Middletown, DE
21 February 2018